During its nearly one hundre[...] [...]out the public about environmental [...] [...]e Earth dubon Society has rarely a[...] Books portant as reaching out to the world's young people, the voices of tomorrow. For Audubon and its 600,000 members, nothing is so crucial as ensuring that those voices speak in the future on behalf of wildlife.

Audubon reaches out to people in many ways—through its nationwide system of wildlife sanctuaries, through research vital to helping set the nation's environmental policy, through lobbying for sound conservation laws, through television documentaries and fact-based dramatic films, through *Audubon* magazine and computer software, and through ecology workshops for adults and Audubon Adventures clubs in school classrooms. Each of these is critical to reaching a large audience. And now, with the Audubon One Earth books, the environmental community can speak to the young minds in our citizenry.

Aubudon is proud to publish One Earth in cooperation with Delacorte Press. In addition to bringing new information and experiences to young readers, these books will instill in them a fundamental concern for the environment and its decline at the hands of humanity. They will also, it is hoped, stimulate an undying interest in the natural world that will empower young people, as they mature, to protect the world's natural wonders for themselves and for future generations.

We at Audubon hope you will enjoy the One Earth books and that you will find in them an inspiration for joining our earth-saving mission. Young people are the hope for our future.

Christopher N. Palmer
Executive Editor
President, National Audubon
Society Productions

ONE EARTH

SAVE OUR WETLANDS

RON HIRSCHI

Photographs by Erwin and Peggy Bauer

National
Audubon
Society

DELACORTE PRESS/NEW YORK

If you would like to receive more information about the National Audubon Society write to:

National Audubon Society, Membership Department,
700 Broadway, New York, New York 10003

Executive Editor: Christopher N. Palmer

Published by
Delacorte Press
Bantam Doubleday Dell Publishing Group, Inc.
1540 Broadway
New York, New York 10036

Library of Congress Cataloging in Publication Data

Hirschi, Ron
    Save our wetlands / by Ron Hirschi ; photographs by Erwin and
Peggy Bauer.
        p.   cm.—(One earth)
    "National Audubon Society."
    Includes index.
    ISBN 0-385-31152-4.—ISBN 0-385-31197-4 (pbk.)
    1. Wetland ecology—United States—Juvenile literature.
2. Wetlands—United States—Juvenile literature. 3. Wetland
conservation—United States—Juvenile literature.   [1. Wetlands.
2. Wetland ecology.   3. Ecology.]   I. Bauer, Erwin A., ill.
II. Bauer, Peggy, ill.   III. Title.   IV. Series: Hirschi, Ron.   One earth.
QH104.H553   1994
574.5'26325'0973—dc20   93-4984   CIP   AC

This edition is published simultaneously in a
Delacorte Press hardcover edition and a
Delacorte Press trade paperback edition.

Manufactured in the United States of America

March 1994

10 9 8 7 6 5 4 3 2 1

For Holly,
Susan, and
Young Shawn

Contents

Introduction

Water, a precious natural resource and a necessity for all life, covers four fifths of our earth. We are surrounded by it everywhere we go. As bodies of water meet the ground around them, both give way to a most precious type of habitat—wetlands. Wetlands, rivers, and streams ooze with life, offering homes to fish, frogs, herons, and other wildlife. They also serve as critical links to other habitats, providing food and shelter for species that use wet places only during a particular time in their life.

Wetlands are extremely valuable. Ducks cannot live without them, many fish depend on them for survival, and some of our rarest birds, including the magnificent whooping crane, need them in order to continue living on the planet.

Not only are wetlands and streams intimately tied to the species that permanently or temporarily inhabit them, but they are also tied to surrounding lands. They need woodlands and meadows near them, just as you need friends. The plants that flourish there trap pollutants that would otherwise flow into the water. These plants are much more than a protective shield, however. Visit a stream or wetland and sit quietly for a while and you will see birds flying back and forth from dry areas into wet ones. While the wetlands provide a rich feeding ground, the trees offer places to nest or roost.

Despite their high value, wetlands are rapidly disappearing. As human populations grow and cities expand, wetlands are covered to make way for homes, offices, factories, and shopping centers. In farming country, wetlands are filled with soil to extend fields. The vegetation along small streams as well as along rivers is continually cut down, removing a valuable part of the ecosystem. Laws and promises from government to protect wetlands are often broken. It will take strong leadership, in both government and in your communities, to save our wetlands from destruction.

This book will show you many examples of wildlife that are dependent on wetlands as well as on rivers and streams. It will also give you a sense of the wide variety of wetlands that exist in our country and how they and other habitats are interconnected. These are not just areas where water collects on the ground or flows across the land. These wet places are filled with life. They are fun to visit just for sightseeing, but they are also great places to fish, catch frogs, search for turtles, or follow dragonflies as they zip back and forth across the water's surface.

No matter where you live—in the city or the country—there is a small wetland, a stream, or a marsh that you can help protect. And within its boundaries, you can find lots of life that needs your help, too. In order for you to understand wet places and their inhabitants better, let's start by getting to know one of the most widespread examples, the freshwater marsh.

SAVE OUR WETLANDS

T he freshwater marsh is a wetland where some open water is visible, but where most of the area is covered with low-growing plants. Water lilies and cattails are common, as well as grasslike plants such as sedges and rushes. A few woody shrubs and trees might grow in the marsh, but most of the plant life is soft, bending when a blackbird lands or when the wind blows.

Even the open water of the marsh can be covered with tiny plants. Duckweed is like a miniature version of a lily pad with a leaf about as big as a pencil eraser is wide. Because it is not grounded in soil, duckweed sprouts a slender root that gathers food and moisture from the water. It floats on the surface, forming pale green mats made of thousands of individual plants.

Cattails and tall rushes live in wet ground at the marsh's edge and extend into the water. Like trees, they offer animals a place to hide and nest. Among the cattails the red-winged blackbird sings, and in another part of the country, its relative, the yellow-headed blackbird, also nests in cattail marshes.

The marsh is not just a valuable wildlife home. It acts like a giant sponge, soaking up water that flows across the land. Over the years, mucky soil known as peat forms beneath the marsh. This wet layer stores moisture that is slowly released, as the days turn drier. Any land downhill from the marsh benefits.

The marsh also stores water that gradually seeps down into the earth, where it forms large pools called aquifers.

Freshwater Marshes

1

According to the Environmental Protection Agency (EPA), 45 percent of all animals and 26 percent of plants listed as federally endangered or threatened species in the United States depend on wetlands. Whooping cranes, crocodiles, and other species must have wetland habitat to survive. How much do we have, and how much have we lost?

Wetlands covered about 200 million acres when Europeans first settled in the United States. More than half—some 100 million acres of wetland habitat—has been lost to date.

Wetlands are continually drained, filled, plowed, and dumped into with fewer restrictions than just a few years ago. Strong leadership is needed to encourage greater protection. You can learn more about what is being done by writing to the EPA, Office of Wetlands Protection, (A-104F), 401 M Street S.W., Washington, D.C. 20460.

These underground water reservoirs provide much of our drinking water. So marshes not only sustain wildlife; they help replenish well water that people drink each day.

Marshes also help keep water clean as their plants trap sediments and many kinds of pollutants, such as oil products. This does not mean that the marsh and its inhabitants can accept lots of pollutants. The food chain would likely become contaminated. However, many developing areas have found that the marsh can be used for some forms of pollution cleaning, including the filtering of sewage wastes. There will always be some damage to the marsh as pollutants flow into wetlands, but some contaminants are more acceptable as they can be chemically broken down into harmless components. The key to ensuring a marsh's well-being is to observe and sample them so problems don't build up.

Once people recognize the tremendous value of marshes, they will surely want to save them. By soaking up excess water they prevent flooding. By trapping pollutants, they are a natural water cleanser. Arm yourself and others with the facts so that if you discover a freshwater marsh that is being destroyed, you'll be prepared to protect this special place.

Frogs

For many people, the sound of spring peepers signals the end of winter. These small eastern frogs, who call in the change of seasons, need the wetlands to survive as do countless other frogs found throughout the United States. Their skin is slippery, as you know if you have tried to catch one of these sleek little jumpers. It must be kept moist since infections can quickly occur if the outer layer becomes dry. Should a frog's skin remain dry for a long period of time, the frog can actually die. This is why frogs live in wetlands or in damp woods near streams or ponds. This is also why frogs disappear when their habitats are altered or destroyed by land development and pollution.

WETLAND PLANTS

Wade along the shallow edge of a marsh or pond. Gently lift floating plants and brush your hand across the surface of others that grow up and out of the water. Notice any differences between these wetland plants and those growing in the nearby fields or woods?

You won't find thorns, and rarely will wetland plants be anything other than soft and crunchy-firm, almost like a piece of celery. Maybe that is why they are in such demand as wildlife food. Wetland plants are among the most productive in nature. They take in lots of food from the water flowing in and around them, and from the rich mucky soil beneath them, which is constantly replenished as water washes more nutrients into the wetland.

Sedges, rushes, cattails, and water lilies are some familiar examples of wetland plants. You can learn about them and others from local field guides that are available in many states. Borrow one from the library, or buy one at the bookstore. Visit a marsh and identify some of the plants, then watch for wildlife users. Do marsh wrens choose a certain kind of plant for nesting? Will deer munch more often on a certain kind of leaf? Can you tell what marsh-plant seeds ducks are eating? Check out the following book for a starting point in conducting your own studies: *American Wildlife and Plants, A Guide to Wildlife Food Habits* by Martin, Zim, and Nelson, published by Dover.

So, what good are frogs? Why do we need them? You can probably come up with many answers to these questions, but the most basic is that all life is sacred and connected to all other life. This belief is shown to be true again and again during scientific studies. We know that frogs consume many insects we don't like to have around, such as mosquitoes. The frogs, in turn, become food for great blue herons, river otters, raccoons, largemouth bass, loons, kingfishers, and other wildlife.

Frogs are also one of the best indicators we have of the general state of the earth. Many scientists believe that frogs are issuing a global warning to humankind. Frogs can tell us when the land is injured, or when the air is unclean. Visit

Because wetlands are so valuable, they are protected by local, state, and federal laws. All of these regulations require that the wetland be defined. Lines must be drawn marking which area is upland (any area supporting mostly dryland plants), which is wetland. But where does the wetland begin?

Wetland specialists and others who try to save wetlands often get into battles almost as fierce as wars—over drawing lines. This is particularly true if a property owner whose line happens to cross a wetland proposes new uses for the land.

If there is muck and mud, drippy plants, and frogs hopping out from under your feet, there is no question that this is wetland. But as you move away from the muddiest places where water does not stand above the ground, the wetland's border becomes difficult to define. This is especially true in places and during times of the year when drought conditions prevail. If the climate has been dry for a number of years, the wetland may actually look like a very parched place.

Two things help identify a wetland under tough conditions. One is soil. There are certain kinds of soils that develop in wetlands, and a trained specialist can identify them easily. Wetland plants are also indicators of the habitat as they often remain the dominant vegetation even through long periods of drought. The soil and the plants draw a line that shows us clearly where this sensitive habitat begins and ends. Once the boundaries are established, the wetland can be saved from property owners and developers.

their habitat and listen for their song. If you don't hear them where you have before, their absence is a signal that the environment is in trouble. The frogs are no longer present because the wetland could not support them. Frogs have vanished from Central American rain forests as well as from some regions of the United States. Worldwide, alarming reports of decreasing frog populations have led scientists to study frog distribution and abundance to try to determine if habitat problems are the cause. Some problems that affect frogs may affect people.

Like scientists, you can take field notes on frog populations, too. Besides conducting frog counts, you can also record their sounds with a tape recorder. Counts can be taken simply by writing down the number of frogs seen within a given length of time. You might ask your teacher to let your class participate in frog counts. Some research money is available for this work, so you should contact your state wildlife agency.

When you do a frog census, remember that these amphibians are valuable in the places they live. Their populations have been harmed by overcollecting, so keep your frog or frog-egg gathering at a minimum. A few frogs are great for aquarium observations, but if we take too many from their homes, they will vanish, just as they do from pollution.

If frogs are abundant in the marsh you visit, the air and water quality are probably good. If there seems to be a shortage of frogs, it is time to improve the air and water. Since frogs can tell us about the quality of the environment, keep an eye and an ear alert for changes at your nearest marsh.

Salamanders

Scientists are concerned about frog populations, but they are even more worried about salamanders. Many of them live in two worlds, moving back and forth between uplands and wetlands. They come into a marsh to breed, then crawl up into the forest to feed, search for a safe shelter, or spend the winter. Destruction of either habitat is fatal to them.

Like frogs, salamanders also serve as environmental indicators, and they suffer from both air and water pollution. Many of them must maintain a moist skin layer since they breathe through their skin. Conditions that dry their bodies are harmful, but sometimes wet areas can be dangerous, too. Acid rain (rainfall that includes acids from car exhaust and other pollutants such as factory smoke) already has affected salamander populations. Eggs and young are especially vul-

DISAPPEARING FROGS AND TOADS

Scientists around the world have been reporting frog disappearances. In the United States, many of the population declines occur in the West. Here are some alarming facts:

Cascade Mountains frog populations have shown a 20 to 40 percent decline in Oregon.

The red-legged frog has not been seen in the Willamette Valley of Oregon for 20 years.

The spotted frog, once abundant in the Cascade Mountains of Washington and Oregon, is now gone from that area.

Three species of yellow-legged frogs have declined in California.

The Yosemite toad was once abundant in the mountains of California but is now declining.

California red-legged frogs are disappearing.

The Las Vegas leopard frog and the San Felipe leopard frog are both extinct.

5

nerable to increases in acidity, and this air pollution problem is seen as a serious threat.

Unfortunately, areas with high levels of acid rain also tend to receive high levels of other pollutants. Heavy metals such as lead often fall with the acid, and the combination of these pollutants can harm salamanders as well as other marsh inhabitants. Predators of the salamanders, such as herons, fish, and loons, also take in the pollutants. In this way, the effects of pollution are quickly spread through the entire food chain.

Salamander populations are even being affected by pollution in many areas you might not suspect. Researchers have shown, for example, that tiger salamanders in the Rocky Mountains of Colorado declined by 65 percent during seven years in the 1980s. Their studies indicate the declines were due to acid rain and that the population may be headed for extinction.

Use a field guide to amphibians to search for salamanders in your region. Conduct surveys in wooded areas near a marsh as well as in the wetlands, taking note of young salamanders as well as adults. Your surveys should span several years to take into account changes over time. This may seem difficult or impossible, but it is important research that can make a difference. You could ask your teacher to let your class start a survey that can be continued by each class after yours for many years. You can also conduct a survey in this way through your Girl or Boy Scout troop or other clubs. Your discoveries can help open eyes to the threats of widespread pollution problems.

Ducks

Mallards, pintails, canvasback, black ducks, teal, and redheads . . . all of these ducks share several things in common. They depend on the freshwater marshes for food, resting habitat, and shelter. Most make their nests within the thick marsh plants lining small ponds or lakes. They also share losses in population, mostly due to the destruction of wetlands caused by droughts, pollution, or development.

In the mid-1980s, biologists began noticing alarming declines in some of the most common and abundant ducks. In 1985 the mallard population had dwindled by as much as 35 percent, while pintails declined by 50 percent. Ducks such as the redhead were already doing poorly because of their specialized need for deep-water marshland and were down almost another 20 percent below previously perilous numbers.

Ducks are especially dependent on breeding wetland habitat in the northern United States and in the Canadian prairie provinces. Once, these vast prairies were sprinkled with thousands upon thousands of small marshes known as potholes. These tiny but numerous water-filled depressions supported millions of ducks that flew north during migration to lay eggs and raise their young. Many of the potholes have been filled as farmers have increased their plowable land. In recent years, drought conditions have dried still more of the valuable wetlands.

Land surrounding the pothole breeding grounds is also valuable habitat. Tall prairie grasses and plants that grow in wet soil typically grow in denser clumps or reach a taller size than plants in dry soil. This vegetation once offered young ducks a place to hide from predators such as coyotes, hawks, or golden eagles. Now, farmers typically plow to the edge of the wetland, even if the pothole is spared filling or draining. The result is almost as damaging as if the wetlands were destroyed, since waterfowl, especially young ducks, are more vulnerable to predation because of the lack of cover.

In Pacific U.S. coastal areas, an estimated 90 percent of the wetlands have already been lost due to agricultural draining or filling. This marsh loss has had a devastating impact on ducks, and one of the most dramatic examples was dis-

FROG SYMPHONY WITH A CHORUS OF LOONS

You have probably heard nature recordings that are now sold in many shops and catalogs. To help raise awareness of the wetlands in the area in which you live, why not make recordings of your own?

Frogs, loons, blackbirds, and the sounds of fish splashing all make beautiful music. A small, hand-held tape recorder is all you need, though more expensive equipment can allow you to pinpoint certain sounds or locations.

One of the best ways to make a nature recording is to put your tape player in a good spot, turn it on, and then leave. Just make sure it is in a dry place! Try recording both in early morning and late afternoon, as well as during times when the weather is not so great. The sound of rain may make you want to stay indoors, but it is a great accompaniment.

Even ducks are music-makers, especially goldeneyes. Many people call them "whistlers" for the sound their wings make when they rush past in flight. Ducks quacking, fishermen casting their lines, and paddles striking the water can also be part of the symphony you record. Wetlands are places for people to enjoy not only for the sights but for their beautiful sounds, too.

covered in California's San Joaquin Valley in the early 1980s. There the Kesterson National Wildlife Refuge offered a winter and nesting habitat for thousands of ducks and other birds. Water flowing into Kesterson Refuge was drained from agricultural areas where the soil had naturally high levels of selenium. This element is toxic to animals even at very low levels. Drainage canals concentrated the selenium-enriched waters, and as they flooded into the vast marshes of Kesterson, the wildlife began to suffer. The water was also unsafe for humans, and the supply had to be cut off, destroying the marsh habitat.

Throughout the United States, similar problems exist for freshwater marshes that may be smaller and less famous than those at Kesterson National Wildlife Refuge. When we allow water contaminated with pollutants to flow directly into our wetlands, ducks are often among the first to suffer.

You can help save freshwater marsh habitats, and there are many people and organizations willing to give you assistance. Because more and more people and government agencies are recognizing the values of wetlands, chances are there is a wetland conservation group in your neighborhood you can join. Contact your local planning agency, the National Audubon Society, Nature Conservancy, or Ducks Unlimited. If none of these groups is conducting a wetland survey, begin one of your own. Get to know the plants and animals present, and take note of any forms of pollution. Unfortunately, wetlands are often neglected until they are in immediate danger; so if you spot a problem, such as the presence of oil on the water, call a state official or local environmental group immediately.

Whooping Cranes

Like Jackie Robinson's rookie-year baseball card, whooping cranes are rare treasures of lasting value. But today, it is difficult to predict just how long the birds will last.

These tall, white, wading cranes with black tips on their wings are inhabitants of the wetlands, and their survival depends on the preservation of their habitat. Whooping cranes require freshwater wetlands for nesting, and a very special kind of wetland—the salt marsh—for the winter.

Although the whooping crane population has increased in the past 50 years, the bird is still endangered. There were only 29 whooping cranes left on earth in 1937 when a refuge was established for them in their Texas wintering grounds. The total population today stands at 131.

Currently, whooping cranes spend their winter in the coastal marshlands of Texas, then fly north to Wood Buffalo National Park in Canada for the summer. It is in the northern marshes of Canada that future generations of whoopers are born. Although the Texas population of the cranes has been saved, new fears have mounted for the preservation of the habitat they need to survive.

The salt-marsh habitat within their Aransas refuge, for instance, is vanishing. Approximately 230 acres of the refuge have eroded in recent years at a rate as high as 4 acres each year. The marsh is located off the Texas coast, but it used to be more completely protected by barrier islands sitting offshore. In the 1940s, a channel was dug between the barrier islands and the refuge. This channel permits boat traffic to travel more safely within the protected waterway, but it keeps getting wider as water swirls against the shore, eroding the marsh. Muck dredged out of the channel to keep it deep enough for boats has also been dumped on the refuge. Heaps of it now cover the former marshland.

Fortunately, the whooping cranes have many friends. The National Audubon Society has been working to force improvements in the way the U.S. Army Corps of Engineers manages the channel running through the Aransas refuge. This agency dug the channel and is responsible for main-

9

taining it. People who live near the cranes are also helping out in a big way. Local residents in the Corpus Christi area near Aransas have begun protecting whooping crane marshland by stacking sandbags to reinforce the shorelines. Some say it will take at least $1 million to do what is needed to protect the area. That money will have to come from Congress—or from a million paper cranes: Imagine if one million people folded a $1 bill into the shape of this elegant yet endangered bird and sent their contributions to a crane-saving organization. Maybe you will be the first to do so.

Farther north, people also work to protect crane habitat in areas where the birds migrate. You can also help these efforts. Trace the path of whooping cranes to Canada and your line will cross most of the center of our country. Write to the governor's office in South Dakota, Nebraska, and Oklahoma to find out what those states are doing to protect crane marshlands.

Sandhill Cranes

Magnificent dancers, the sandhill cranes are among the most spectacular of all wetland birds. Freshwater marsh is the habitat they prefer, especially to nest. Though they have not suffered as severely as the larger and more visible whooping crane, sandhills are not as widely scattered across the country as before.

Gray or brown feathered, the sandhills wear a bright red cap. With long legs and a long beak, they wade or stalk freshwater marshes in search of frogs, mice, insects, and other prey. At the beginning of the breeding season, pairs dance as they call in loud, rattling songs. Jumping off the ground, they spread their wings and strut in a ritual performance that can be heard—and seen—from a great distance. Tall and lanky, the sandhill has a wingspread of just under seven feet. At the turn of the century, they were hunted in large numbers, and populations declined severely. Surprisingly, they are still hunted today in several areas of the West.

During winter and migration, the sandhills gather in large flocks, the largest on a section of the Platte River in Nebraska. This migratory stopover is one of the grand spectacles for wildlife viewers, since as many as 500,000 cranes congregate in this area during the spring migration. Seeing so many cranes at one time renews the spirit and encourages the thought that people have done a great job to save wildlife. The National Audubon Society and the Platte River Whooping Crane Trust can be thanked for protecting much of the crane habitat. The rare whoopers also use these areas in their migration, though whooping cranes continue farther north than the majority of the sandhills.

Although the Platte River harbors so many sandhills today, it once supported significantly more birds. Because of habitat alteration, only a remnant 80-mile stretch of Platte River wetland is available now to the cranes, while more than 300 miles were sandhill habitat in previous years. More severe losses have been recorded in other states. The sandhill is an endangered species in Ohio, for instance, and in Washington State only one may be left. As river water is diverted to irrigate agricultural fields, lake shores are built upon, and wetlands are filled, loss of water affects wildlife and wetland habitat. Again, using the Platte River as an example, farmers use 70 percent of the river's water for irrigation. The river drops, and all of the wetlands along the banks and in its valley also dry up.

Once water levels drop significantly, wildlife populations decline. Sometimes, out of laziness or disregard, we simply accept these new lower levels as normal or natural. Talk to your grandparents or other people who have lived in your area for a long time. You might discover that wildlife populations were much higher in years past. Instead of being passive and accepting things as they are, maybe we can put

11

some of the water back into the rivers. Maybe we can restore some of the wetlands. Then wildlife populations will increase and become more sustainable over time. Wouldn't it be wonderful if a million sandhill cranes danced on the Platte each spring!

S wamps are drippy, swamps are tangled, swamps are the places where you will find so much life you will never be disappointed. But somehow swamps have either gotten a bad name or they just don't register high in the public appreciation poll. Despite their incredible richness, swamps have disappeared as completely and as quickly as any wetland habitat, and with them have gone some wonderful animals.

In the days when Europeans first settled America, swamps filled river bottomlands, bordering the streams and spreading out in low areas where rivers flood. The greatest of these was along the Mississippi River. Like all swamps, this river-bottom wetland was forested. The presence of trees distinguishes a swamp from a marsh. There may or may not be standing water in a swamp, but the trees can tolerate wet soil and can even tolerate being flooded from time to time.

About 25 million acres of bottomland forest in the Mississippi region once provided homes for bears, deer, wood ducks, and other wildlife, which you still can see today. However, since people have cut down all but a few million acres of this wetland forest, you will never see one of its occupants, the ivory-billed woodpecker, again. And the red wolves that once inhabited this area are nearly gone, too.

The kinds of trees found in a swamp vary from region to region, with the greatest variety in the East and Southeast. Some of our most extensive swamps remain in these regions today. Despite the tremendous losses of the past, in some swamps you can still hear or see almost all the wildlife these areas once supported.

One of America's — and the earth's — most magnificent wetlands, the Everglades of southern Florida is home to many of our most unusual wildlife, as well as to hundreds of those found in wetlands elsewhere. The Everglades has been called a river of grass because of the way water flows across the tall marsh plants. Here and there the marsh is broken by raised clusters of trees where spoonbills, herons, and prothonotary warblers can be seen. Alligators, frogs, turtles, and cougars live in the wilds of the wetland. Crocodiles survive in the coastal fringes of the area protected within Everglades National Park.

The Everglades has changed dramatically over the years. Half of it is gone, having been filled, drained, or cleared, and the 4.5 million people who live at its edges continually threaten its future. Farmers, especially those growing sugarcane, actually use the wetland, and pump water from sources that used to flow into it. Water is also pumped away from the Everglades to supply cities that have increasing water needs.

Water loss has dried sections of the Everglades, while water diversion has dramatically altered wetlands in other parts of Florida. This is especially true where the once-meandering Kissimmee River has been straightened into a canal. Since runoff into the canal contains agricultural wastes, people are just beginning to complain about the problems facing the lake where the canal deposits the polluted water. If action is taken to correct this problem, it may help return the Kissimmee to its former meandering route. Dozens of environmental groups are now calling for greater efforts to restore natural water flows into the Everglades — to bring wetness back to this incredibly valuable habitat.

The swamps that do exist today still offer valuable habitat. Since marsh plants and trees grow in their midst, the swamp is a combination of habitats. They provide food and shelter to animals needing a wet home and housing to those that nest, roost, or feed in trees. Swamps are especially valuable to large, tree-nesting water birds such as herons. Like the marshes, swamps also provide important services for people, such as filtering and storing water.

The very word *swamp* often suggests a negative place for people. Others, like yourself, know the beauty and value of swamps. Visit some of our wooded wetlands soon and help spread the word that swamps—and their wildlife—aren't so bad!

Wood Storks

Like many birds that need swamp habitat, the wood stork also can be seen in more open, nonwooded wetlands. They

---

TULE ELK AND SWAMP RABBITS

Wetland wildlife are usually adapted to live most, if not all, of their lives in and around water. Ducks have webbed feet, frogs can breathe underwater, and cranes have long legs for wading in the shallows. A few mammals can live in water, including the beaver, muskrat, and otter. And you may be surprised by the other species that do well here, too.

Swamp rabbits take to water like ducks. They readily jump into ponds or rivers, swimming to avoid danger or to get from place to place. They live mainly in the lowlands, where they prefer to eat wetland plants such as sedges. Swamp rabbits also dive underwater, a habit that is shared by few other mammals.

Tule elk historically occupied swampy areas and other lowlands of central and coastal California. Unlike the related Rocky Mountain and Roosevelt elk, they prefer the lowlands even though they can survive at higher, drier elevations.

Originally, about 500,000 tule elk inhabited the California lowlands. Centered in San Francisco, trade in meat, hide, and tallow from the elk soon depleted their herds during the middle 1800s. By the mid-1800s, elk had disappeared north of San Francisco Bay. Marshes were drained throughout the remainder of their range, and by the 1870s, the tule elk was nearly extinct.

Today, a few hundred tule elk survive in isolated herds, but their wetland habitat is mostly gone. Like ducks or beaver taken from water, they can survive, but they will never be the same animals over time; the wetland, like any animal's home, is a part of what they have become.

---

feed in marshes and in farm fields or pastures that are wet. But the stork needs a swamp for nesting, and they have preferences for where they do put their nests.

With a wingspread of about five feet, the large-bodied wood stork needs big trees for nest building. At one time, they could find nesting habitat within the Southeast from Texas to South Carolina. Now suitable habitat remains mostly in Florida, where they place their nests in mangroves, cypress, buttonwood, and custard-apple trees. In some years, they can be found in Georgia and the Carolinas—hopefully, this will continue.

But generally, wood stork nesting and their overall population have declined over the years. This is due to a loss of feeding habitat near the swamps where they once nested in large numbers. Changes in the flow of water into the Everglades has made it much harder for wood storks to catch fish during the nesting season. Without this feeding habitat, the swamp nest sites can still be valuable for other birds but not for the storks.

Single colonies in Florida once contained more than 15,000 pairs of wood storks. Recent estimates place the total population below 10,000 pairs.

Wood Ducks

Wood ducks are incredibly beautiful. The red-eyed male wears a crest splashed with blue and green feathers tinged with irridescent sparkles. At the turn of the century, hunters nearly caused their extinction. Today, laws protect the wood duck from being overhunted, and it is again a common bird in many areas.

Unlike the wood stork, the wood duck both nests and feeds in wooded swamps. With its smaller body size, it can slip into spaces within trees and swamp tangles to search for food. Like the wood stork, this duck needs trees for nesting, and it, too, has suffered decreases in its population because of the loss of habitat.

Wood ducks nest in tree cavities, often in old woodpecker homes or in a natural crevice. They also readily accept nesting boxes, which you may have seen in the middle of small ponds or in shallow water along a lakeshore. Wherever old trees have disappeared, nesting boxes can temporarily replace a part of the swamp habitat. Although some birds, such as the wood duck, will nest in these artificial homes, it is wise to protect the natural swamp habitat. This ensures a perpetual supply of nests and preserves the many other features provided by wetland trees.

Because wood ducks are easily attracted to nest boxes and are fairly tolerant of people, you can encourage them to nest near your home, even in the middle of a city. Many bird books provide plans for building a nest box. Build your own box and begin looking for a suitable wood duck habitat. Your search may lead you to help re-create or protect some valuable wetland habitat.

Wood ducks need access to open water, but they will build their nests away from wet vegetation or standing water. You can place your box in water or as far away as 100 yards; situate it at least 5 feet above the water or ground. Amazingly, wood ducks will nest as high above the ground as 40 feet. Downy young will drop to the ground without harm when they are ready to leave the nest.

Wood ducks feed on lots of different plant parts, including the seeds of land and water plants. They eat acorns, duckweed, sedge and rush seeds, wigeon grass, beechnuts, wild rice, and smartweed as well as other plants. Sometimes they will eat animals, such as a frog, and aquatic insects, such as dragonflies, mayflies, beetles, and mosquitoes.

To maintain or promote a healthy habitat for wood ducks, all the food sources must be available. In general, this requires a wetland with clean water surrounded by lush as well as tall vegetation. If your duck-nesting area has been cleared of trees, one of the simplest things you can do is to plant some varieties that are tolerant of getting their roots wet. You can research these trees in local field guides and by visiting wetlands and identifying the trees growing at their edge or within the standing water.

Black Bears and Bobcats

Usually thought of as forest animals, the black bear and bobcat also depend on swamps for survival. The landscape of large swamps is very diverse, offering bears and bobcats scattered dry ground. Fallen trees and shallow water provide places to hunt for food. Black bears eat mostly berries, grasses, and plants. They also consume small mammals and insects such as ants. Bobcats feed more on small mammals, birds, and insects.

Because they are large animals, both bears and bobcats disappear as natural habitat begins to shrink in size. Large swamps may serve as refuges, but they will persist only if large forested areas and other natural habitat are protected. This is especially true today in the eastern United States, where a distribution map of both bears and bobcats shows many gaps. Widespread forest clearing and wetland draining have robbed them of their homes. This problem is also accelerating in the West.

We chronicle the loss of wetlands as they disappear year after year. Then one day we wake up to find animals gone that were present just a few years ago. Some of these animals are fairly common today, but it is the large and more predatory type that, even when common, disappear first. Needing more room and more food, they are the first to vanish.

Another problem facing animals such as the black bear is that they can be hard to live with. Large expanses of wetland provide a buffer between them and human hunting and habitation. As more new homes are built in rural areas, including on the edges of swamps, it is increasingly likely that people will come in contact with bears. Few stop to realize that this is the bear's one and only home. Will we be able to save this creature? Can we protect the wetlands that offer refuge to animals like bears and bobcats? If you do know of a swamp where bears and bobcats now thrive, try to keep track of their presence. Your job as bear and bobcat saver can last many years and will help you learn much more about your surroundings. One way to begin is to conduct research that is far safer than actually following bears or bobcats. Write to your state wildlife agency and ask for historical information about bears and bobcats. Try also to find people who have hunted or trapped these animals—ask them where bears and bobcats have vanished. Chances are good that in these instances it is not the hunting that has harmed whole populations of the animals; destroying the swamp habitat kills far more.

Prothonotary Warblers

No one knows how many prothonotary warblers existed in the past, and no one knows how many exist today. They are most commonly found in wooded swamps in the southeastern parts of the United States. Beautifully feathered in gold and yellow, these small birds feed on insects. Unlike most of their relatives, they nest in tree cavities, thus depending on the swamp for both nesting and feeding habitat.

Prothonotary warblers, which migrate to Central and South America in winter, are one example of animals that travel back and forth between our wetlands and those farther south. Many more animals found in our wetlands also occur in more tropical areas. Southern wildlife that finds secure homes in Mexico, Central or South America, as well as in this country include great egrets, little blue herons, cattle egrets, reddish egrets, and wood storks, just to name a few.

Like tropical rain forests, wetlands south of our border are also disappearing. It is just as critical to protect the wetlands needed by southern wildlife as it is to save wintering places used by birds such as the prothonotary warbler. When wetlands are destroyed, the abundance of wildlife as well as their distribution declines. Little by little, their populations drop. Once below critical levels, they vanish just as rain forest wildlife vanishes.

Perhaps you could help begin efforts to protect these habitats. Wetlands certainly rank high on a list of places to protect. This is true in tropical America as well as in Asia and Africa, where agricultural draining of wetlands destroys many thousands of acres of critical wildlife habitat. The time to protect tropical wetlands has come.

Male and Female Cinnamon Teal

Northern Leopard Frog

Male Pintail

Alligator

Snowy Egret

Bogs

Discover a bog, and you will have discovered some of the most unusual members of the plant world. But you will have to get down on your hands and knees to look closely. Many of the best views of the bog are close to the mossy surface of the wetland.

The first thing you will notice if you do walk out onto a bog is that the ground beneath your feet seems to tremble. It is almost like a huge waterbed! Bogs develop as sphagnum moss forms mats of slow-growing vegetation in ponds, lakes, or marshes. This sphagnum mat blocks water movement, and as the moss and other bog plants die, a layer of slowly decomposing vegetation, the peat layer, begins to form. Shrubs, trees, and other plants can take root in the peat. Water surrounding the sphagnum is more acidic than that where the moss is absent, a condition that many plants cannot tolerate. Nitrogen is also limited, and the combined effect is an environment where very special bog plants thrive.

Pitcher plants, sundew, and bladderwort are bog-dwelling plants that eat insects or small aquatic animals. Each has specialized in predation to deal with unique conditions within the bog. Watching these plants is a fascinating lesson in wetland survival techniques.

Insects are eaten by predatory bog plants in part as a response to the lack of nutrients in the sphagnum-influenced peat soil. The pitcher plant catches its prey in tall, tubular leaves that come complete with an attractor—a hooded opening that draws insects. Inside the tube, tiny hairs point downward, preventing the insects from climbing out if they fall in. Water gathers at the base of the tube, and this liquid is used by the pitcher plant to digest its meals.

Sundew plants are a little more straightforward in their predatory behavior. Their leaves are covered with little hairlike projections coated with a sticky, gluelike secretion. Insects that land on sundew plants may be unable to take off again.

The tiny bladderwort plants work beneath the water to capture their prey. Rootlike appendages spread below the surface to catch aquatic animals within tiny bladders equipped with trapdoors. Like the pitcher plant and sundew, the bladderwort then digests its prey.

Bog plants that feed in typical plant fashion include bog laurel, Labrador tea, cranberry, and many trees that also grow in upland forests. Because of the acidity and differences in nutrients available, trees found in bogs typically grow much slower than those in a forest. For example, hemlock trees that would normally be more than 70 feet tall have been found to grow only 5 to 6 feet in bogs where they have lived for more than 50 years.

The greatest threat to bogs, in addition to the draining and filling that occurs in other wetlands, comes from the mining of peat. The peat you see in bags at the garden, grocery, or variety store is often excavated from bogs. Valued as a soil additive, the peat is removed from the bog after the surface layer of plants is stripped away, damaging the wetland.

Bog plants are also threatened by people who collect them for indoor gardening at home. This is a problem for many other rare and endangered plants, too.

No vertebrates, or animals with backbones, are known to live exclusively in bogs, but many of those found in swamps and marshes also frequent bogs. River otters and beaver are common, as are black bears and raccoons. In Pacific Northwest bogs, a rare beetle, Beller's ground beetle, has been found to live only in these wetlands. But the true beauty of bogs, no matter where they are found, lies in their unique collection of plants adapted to wet and acidic conditions. The damp sphagnum moss, and the bog plants growing within its deep, soft layers, offer a spectacular and small world that is fascinating to explore.

Amazing discoveries reveal themselves beneath the surface of many bogs, too. Because of the acidity and the slow growth of bog plants, as well as the presence of water, decomposition within the peat layer is very, very slow. This peat is often a treasure house of the past. Mastodon skeletons, ancient tools, and boats all have been found preserved in it. The peat layers also give scientists a clear view into past vegetation histories, since layers of pollen collect in it. Bogs help to preserve the past. It is up to us to preserve the bog for the future.

Rivers and Streams

Follow the tiniest trickle of water and it will lead you, eventually, to water that runs as a stream, then a river. Running water is everywhere, and streams will lead you to some of the most exciting wildlife habitats. Getting to know a stream nearby will also acquaint you with wet places that probably need your help.

Throughout our nation, streams big and small have been abused as thoroughly as any habitat. You might think that their saving grace lies in the fact that the water can at least run away from its abuser. Sadly, the rivers and streams we have polluted always carry their problems with them. Each of us lives downstream of someone else who is probably dumping something inappropriate into the water.

Walk along almost any stream bank and you will find visible discards. Pop cans and pop rings, fishing line, old tires, bottles, and other pieces of trash are regularly thrown into running water. Do people think the stream will wash it away permanently?

Unfortunately, the less-visible refuse is more deadly. Lawn chemicals, agricultural sprays, wastewater from cities and towns, and runoff from highways and parking lots all pollute streams. Industrial wastes are also very dangerous and harmful. It is taking people a long time to wake up to the fact that rivers and streams cannot live with these forms of pollution—nor can we.

Part of the problem facing rivers and streams is that much of their life exists below the surface. Until dead fish float to the top, many people would not notice that something is wrong. That is one good reason to become familiar with the many animals of the running waters. Go out and fish in streams and rivers to get to know them as places to have fun, too.

You can learn a lot about a stream by fishing, but there are also other great ways to explore running water. Lots of kids are doing important research into the quality of rivers and streams by exploring a stream on a regular basis. Stream monitoring can take many forms, but the easiest way is to sample its aquatic insects. This can be done simply by picking up rocks and making notes on the kinds of insects living on, and especially under, them. In general, the greater the variety of insects, the higher the water quality.

The kinds of insects present also tell you a lot about how clean your stream happens to be. Mayflies, stoneflies, and caddisflies typically frequent cleaner, clearer water. You can identify these aquatic insects with the help of a field guide. If you want to start monitoring a stream, you should contact your local environmental agency. Often, a biologist will visit your school to help you set up a permanent monitoring program. Biologists can also show you how to use nets and other equipment to capture aquatic insects, crayfish, and other stream animals you will observe in your work.

Many fish and other wildlife depend on our rivers and streams. Aquatic insects form critical food supplies for these animals, but healthy forests and other surrounding habitats also must be present. As you will see in the following examples, many of these nonwetland habitats are often needed to help rivers and streams provide safe homes for most wildlife.

River Otters

River otters have captured many hearts. They are fun to watch and a joy to follow as they swim downstream, run along a riverbank, or dive to snatch a frog, fish, or crayfish. Incredibly good at catching their meals, river otters have lots of time left over to play. They often crawl out onto grassy riverbanks and roll together, grooming one another or stretching out in the sun. They also chase one another on land, in the snow, or in water of any depth.

River otters may be enjoyed for their charming life-style, but they are also valued for their dense, soft fur. Trapped for centuries, river otter populations have been declining in many areas, and they have completely disappeared from some states. Fortunately, they have also been raised in captivity or live-trapped in areas of abundance. These sources of otters have been used successfully to replenish otter populations in other locations.

Otters use streams for many reasons. Sometimes, they will follow the smallest trickle along a streambed with too little water to support food supplies. These tiny streamlets offer the otters a highway to larger streams or to lakes and ponds that can be several miles from where the otters began their journey. But most streams they frequent are traveled and lived in for much, if not all, of the year. Otters might move out of one stream and into another. They will also venture into the open ocean, where they are often mistaken for sea otters, their much larger relatives.

Recent studies have shown that river otters often frequent areas along streams that have marshy, wetland borders. They also travel into lakes and spend lots of time in marshy lake-shore areas. They have been found to disappear from streams with depleted fish populations, even though their diet includes many nonfish prey.

Since they do require healthy fish populations, otters are excellent indicators of a stream's quality. If they are present, chances are the river or stream is clean and productive. When they vanish, it is time to help the stream, taking a close look at its fish population—and its wetlands.

But how do you find otters? Sleek and secretive, they can live along the shores of a lake, marsh, or stream without your even knowing it.

One of the best ways to find otters sounds gross and disgusting, but you have to think like an otter to appreciate this wildlife technique. It's actually one used by many biologists and is called scat telemetry. *Scat* is just another word for feces, and otters use theirs for some important business. They communicate by defecating (passing waste) in very special places they use over and over through the years. One such location at Lake Tahuyah in Washington State is known to have been used for at least 60 years.

Otters swim along the shore, then hop out on a riverbank or other shoreline to rest, feed, or take a nap. Some places where they come ashore are more or less sacred space. They roll around, scrape away plants, and heap little piles of sticks, leaves, and vegetation. Then they poop on top of the little pile, creating a scent mound that carries the otters' odor. That smell is recognized by others and lets otters know if anyone has been around.

Up- and downstream one will find similar spots, and each is marked by otter poop. The scat telemetry technique simply requires finding the spots and visiting them to see if an otter has been present. The poop is very distinctive and usually consists of a pine cone–sized mass of fish bones, crayfish parts, and an occasional feather. It is usually black and a bit fishy smelling. Scientists sift through it the way they sift through owl pellets to find out what the otters have been eating. By scraping away any scat present on a riverbank location, they can also tell when the otters return. Keeping track throughout the year can give valuable information about use of an area through the seasons.

More important, finding a spot where otters regularly come ashore helps identify one small piece of that animal's critical habitat. Otters, like people, have needs that must be met for their survival, and one important need is for a safe place to land. Some of these areas are also dens. Stand on spots where you know otters have been, and beneath your feet there may be a set of tunnels dug by a beaver but now used by otters to raise their young ones.

Otters are probably one of the best wetland indicator species we can use to help protect streams, marshes, and other wet places. Cute like newborn babies, fun loving like little puppies, and elegant swimmers, too, river otters appeal to many people. People seem to love otters in a way they often can't love frogs, turtles, or other wetland animals. In your own campaigns to help save the wetlands, use otters to promote your cause. Draw them, write about them, talk about them, and you might just get results!

Grayling

A dazzling splash of golden spots washed with silver and blue and wide fanlike fins on their backs make grayling look like colorful flying fish. They only lack the long winglike fins of the ocean-dwelling flying fish. If they could, they would probably leap clear of the stream and disappear into the air, they have been so insulted by our destruction of their habitat.

But fish cannot leave water. They must endure our continuous assault. The grayling shows as clearly as any fish can that we aim to keep up our destruction.

Once found in streams throughout the Missouri River headwaters in Montana, in a corner of Wyoming, and in Michigan, the river-dwelling grayling of the lower 48 states is now found mainly in one river, the Big Hole in Montana. Michigan populations probably died as a result of stream impacts from logging. Logging along streams dumps lots of sediment into the water. Since shade trees are gone, the water temperature increases. Logging also changes the amount of water flowing in the stream by reducing the river's watershed,

Tie on a new lure, hook up a heavier sinker, or fasten a swivel to your line. When you go fishing and clip line from the end of your leader or do anything to change gear, you might drop the discarded line to the ground or throw it into the water.

Walk any riverbank or lakeshore and you'll find tangles of line thrown away by anglers. Out in the water, those tangles wrap around the legs of turtles and snarl into nearly invisible nets that capture and kill loons. They also drift onto old logs, forming permanent and anchored nets that kill thousands of wildlife every year.

Just like drift nets in the ocean, fishing line thrown into rivers, streams, and lakes is a killer. You can help by picking up line when you walk along the shore. Don't throw away line that is no longer needed; return it to sporting goods stores that participate in recycling programs.

Fishing line is not the only trash thrown out by anglers. Bait containers made from Styrofoam are common in many areas. Encourage bait salespeople to switch to paper or reusable containers. Place signs near access points, encouraging people to recycle fishing line and bait containers. You might also conduct surveys to find out how much line is discarded along the shore in your area. The amount will probably surprise you and may also shock anglers into changing their ways.

or water-holding ability. If left standing, trees act somewhat like a sponge, slowly releasing water to the stream. If cut, water runs off too quickly.

In Montana, the introduction of nonnative fish into rivers has created problems for native fish like the grayling. These problems include competition for food and living space. Young grayling are also eaten by introduced fish. No problem, however, is as severe as drying up the river. Individual landowners living along streams have the legal right to take water for irrigating their fields or watering livestock. At times, they take so much that very little is left for the fish, certainly not enough for them to survive.

In the past few years, surveys of the Big Hole River have

shown that grayling have declined from 100 fish per mile to about 30. Total population size is estimated to be about 3,000. Fears that the river population faces extinction have encouraged many people to begin working for the grayling's protection, including some landowners.

Young grayling and small trout are often killed in irrigation ditches, channels that divert water away from the river and into farmers' fields. Some landowners are redesigning the way they open their irrigation ditches so they can keep fish from swimming into the fields. Attempts also are being made to buy water from irrigators, but this is an expensive proposition.

A longer-term solution has been in the works for many years, but seems to have little public support. The idea is for biologists to set a minimum flow for each stream. If the water falls below the minimum level, none can be taken. This rule would allow rivers and streams to remain flowing to ensure survival of all its fish and other wildlife. Ecologically, it seems like the right thing to do—rivers should flow, fish should swim.

Unfortunately, rivers will not flow and fish will not swim as long as the water is freely available to individual land-owners. They seem willing to dry up our streams to get water, and the grayling is one example of a loser, as beautiful as they are.

Salmon

Born in stream gravel, tiny salmon wiggle up into the current to begin a life that leads them on one of the most amazing of all journeys. People have studied this journey, marveled at the salmon's great beauty, caught them, eaten them, and have even created cultures nearly completely dependent on these fish. Stories, myths, great art, and wonderful songs tell the tale of the journey of salmon out to sea and back to the streams of their birth.

Returning to Washington's Elwha River for centuries, sockeye salmon would swim to their spawning areas within a small stream that entered the main river. When the sockeye were born, they spent part of their early life in a small lake. Then they swam down the Elwha and out into the sea.

Boys in the Elwha S'Klallam village at the mouth of the Elwha River were once initiated into manhood at this special time of year. While their grandmothers waited, the boys tried to catch a sockeye. When they succeeded, they carried the fish to their grandmother's home, where she would clean it for her grandson. This ritual of catching and cleaning ensured the young man of his passage into manhood. The Elwha S'Klallam depended on this cycle for many centuries.

In the early 1900s, a dam was built across the Elwha River, downstream from the areas where the sockeye salmon came to spawn. Unable to swim above the dam, the sockeye vanished from the area. No more will ever be caught or cleaned, so the rite of passage has been denied for all time.

Chinook, coho, sockeye, chum, and pink salmon of the Pacific Coast and Atlantic salmon of the Northeast share many similar life histories. Each has its special stream requirements, and all share the same fate as rivers are altered by dams, logging, and other activities.

Today, the Atlantic salmon has disappeared from many of its original stream habitats. Pacific salmon have always been significantly more abundant, but they, too, are vanishing. How could they disappear when they once numbered in the millions? Why are salmon in danger?

Probably the best way to understand salmon is to understand the concept of diversity. Diversity is what life is all about. It's the mixing of stuff that is not alike. It's the little differences in things that seem alike. It's needing more than 64 colors in a box of crayons, wanting something new for dinner, or waking up and deciding to wear an outrageous pair of socks.

Streams are diverse because the land makes them that way. Since salmon have adapted to the diversity in streams, they, too, are diverse. Even with one species of salmon there are many types, usually called *stocks* by biologists. Separate stocks of salmon live in different rivers or within tributaries or sections of especially large rivers like the Columbia in the Pacific Northwest. And the Columbia used to be home to so many salmon that if they were all alive and well today, they would outnumber all the Atlantic salmon in all the rivers of the United States. Dams on the mighty Columbia changed all that, though. Today, populations of salmon in the Columbia are only about 5 percent of their original size.

The salmon living in a river the size of the Columbia show clearly how different each separate stock can be from the others. Some chinook salmon swimming down the Columbia and into the Pacific Ocean turn north and into waters off Washington and British Columbia. Others turn south, where they grow to adulthood off the coasts of Oregon and California. The fish don't leave the river at the same time, and each stock adapts to its original area within the stream, the place where it is born. They all return to this same spot to spawn and to die.

Separate stocks of salmon adapted to unique conditions within a stream are needed for long-term survival of the fish. But little by little we have wiped out entire stocks. Recently, biologists have identified a large number of salmon as being endangered. Including steelhead trout (rainbow trout that travel to the ocean and back to streams like salmon), biologists have listed 214 stocks as being in danger, 101 of them at high risk of becoming extinct—soon.

Dams that block fish passage, logging that pollutes streams, overfishing, and destruction of habitat have all contributed to these losses. Another problem that is very controversial is the competition between wild salmon and those produced by hatcheries. Hatcheries have been built to produce salmon in much the same way as cows, chickens, or other livestock are raised. After the little fish are born, they are dumped into rivers and then travel out to sea. But all of these hatchery-produced salmon lack diversity and are often not suited for survival to each stream like the unique and separate stocks of wild fish. They also develop diseases in hatcheries, which they pass along to wild fish in the rivers. Finally, when they are dumped into streams in large numbers, they often eat all the available food. The wild fish, adapted to their home stream so well, are driven away by the hatchery salmon.

How do we save the salmon? On large rivers with dams, the most important thing to do is to make it easier for fish to pass the dams on their downstream and upstream migration. More water needs to be made available for passing fish, either in better-designed fish ladders (structures that help fish climb up and over huge dams that produce electricity) or in other devices. In some places, trucks carry fish around the dams. Of course, removing the dams also is a solution.

Habitat protection is another critical need. Hundreds of miles of salmon streams have been severely altered and continue to be devastated by logging and developing. For salmon, the needs are not as simple as just replanting the stream bank. They need a new generation of people who care about ecosystems—all the river inhabitants and the habitat, too.

Keep your eyes open for chances to write to large landowners who control certain streams. If you read about streams or rivers being altered by logging or other clearing, write to state legislators, to your governor, and to wildlife agencies. Let them know that the health of rivers is important. The list of rivers where salmon are in trouble is a long one. It reads like a legacy of magical places we could still save. In California alone, the rivers with fish in peril include the Sacramento, Klamath, Smith, Yuba, Shasta, Scott, San Joaquin, Mad, Mattole, Russian, Eel, and many small streams. The list for Washington and Oregon would fill this page. Adopt a single one of these streams and you can make a big difference for the future, no matter where you live. Care for the stream, get to know it, visit it someday as if you were making a trip to your most treasured vacation spot.

Visit a salmon stream in fall, put your nose down to the water, and look into the current for a salmon just returned from the sea. A red-sided sockeye glows with color. The broad bands of dark color on a chum flash in the stream's light. Coho seem to reflect the colors of leaves in their beautiful red sides. Pinks form a strange and mystical shape with their humped backs and crooked jaws. Chinooks loom so large you will think a shark is approaching. Each salmon is different from the other, and each has a fascinating history. We can hope that their histories will go on and on.

ADOPT A STREAM

Begun in the Pacific Northwest several years ago, the movement to encourage stream adoption is one of the most successful environmental programs. The idea for adopting streams included the notion that people could protect and even restore salmon populations to streams throughout the Northwest. It has worked.

Stream adoption can be as simple as taking care of your favorite stream all by yourself. Or you can join forces with friends, neighbors, or classmates to adopt a stream that you take care of for a long period of time.

The best place to start is by getting to know your adopted stream. Play in the water, get your feet and knees wet. Forget science and just have fun exploring the stream's banks, turning over its rocks and wading into its quiet pools. You can clean up trash, but remember that streams like to have their own kind of discards.

Old, fallen logs, rocks, and natural debris are valuable stream habitat. Leave them in place since they provide homes for fish, crayfish, turtles, salamanders, and more. Logs even contribute to the food supply of streams; decaying wood is eaten by stream insects that in turn are the food base for many other animals.

With small seine nets, your bare hands, or dip nets, begin to take note of the stream's inhabitants. Compare what you find with field guides to stream life in your area or any historical accounts you can find of your adopted stream. You can begin to restore the stream by consulting biologists from state agencies and conservation organizations who can direct you.

Darters

We have just read about how salmon are in trouble. They decline even though there is a multimillion-dollar fishing industry that depends on these stream dwellers. What kind of interest, then, can be mounted to save a tiny little fish called the darter, about which almost no one knows, from which no person makes any money, and for whose protection no major organization exists?

Maybe darters do have something going for them. Maybe you will take it upon yourself to help them out. After all, they are incredibly beautiful fish with some special habitat needs that we should all pay attention to if we want clean water for our own future.

Darters are more or less the butterflies of streams. Tiny but colorful, they would be photographed, cataloged, and attracted if they lived in air instead of water. Vivid reds and brilliant blues adorn these tiny fish that live in the heartland of our country. The smallest darter is about an inch long, the largest only a little more than six inches. There are about 140 different species that range from Mexico to the Arctic, but most of them live in the Mississippi and its drainages.

Well named, darters are quick swimmers related to perch and walleye. One of the most famous, the snail darter, held up construction of a dam on the Tennessee River in the 1970s. As an extremely rare and endangered fish, the snail darter was threatened with extinction by Tellico Dam, which would destroy its sand and gravel bottom habitat by impounding the river. Ultimately, the dam was constructed, but the fish were temporarily saved when biologists moved snail darters to another river. Since that time, more snail darters have been located in other streams, but their long-term survival is questionable.

The snail darter is in trouble in large part because its populations occur in such a small geographical area. Many other darters are also concentrated in specific areas, such as the emerald darter, which is considered threatened in Tennessee; the riverweed darter of North Carolina; and the sharphead darter, which is considered rare and endangered in Tennessee as well as North Carolina.

One of the most endangered of all darters, the fountain darter, is so limited in its distribution that any single impact could drive it to extinction almost overnight. The fountain darter is found only in a spring at the head of the San Marcos River of Texas and within a two-mile stretch of its stream.

Black Bear Cub

Wood Duck

Beaver

Racoon

River Otter

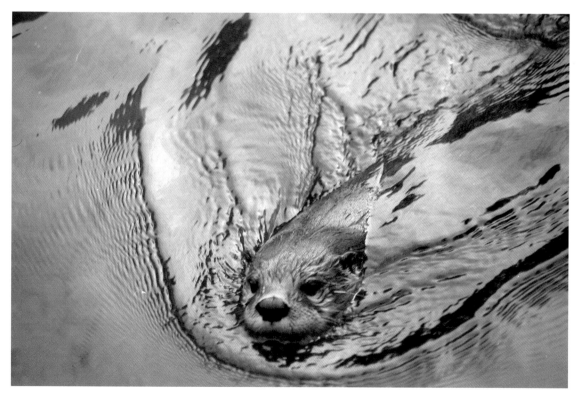

Sockeye Salmon

You should watch for one of the most abundant darters, the rainbow, in your own stream surveys. Like frogs, they are also great indicators of stream health in rivers where human activities gradually alter water quality. Rainbow darters like small gravel areas with a bit of a riffle to them—places where the stream drops a bit and the water is broken by the rocky bottom. Riffles add oxygen to streams as the water tumbles over stones. When people alter streams, by straightening, widening, or deepening them, areas are often lost and with them go the darters.

Natural streams tend to be diverse, and within a stream, just like within a forest, animals select their own special spots. Rainbow darters like riffles, while bluegills like quiet water. Riffles are where stoneflies and caddisflies are abundant; quiet water is a place for damselflies and dragonflies.

You might not catch them on hook and line, but you can scoop up rainbow and other darters with your bare hands or with a small net. Start catching and carefully releasing them if you live from Minnesota to western New York, or Missouri to West Virginia. Keep track of their presence in streams near your home or school, and sound the alarm if they begin to disappear. You will know when you catch one—it is like holding a rainbow in your hands.

Beaver

Although it is not in danger of extinction, the beaver is symbolic of our treatment of rivers and river life. Like the buffalo, they were killed by the thousands from colonial times and during the 1800s as the West was settled. Today, they are still trapped for their thick fur but are generally ignored even though they contribute significantly to the shape of our water world.

Master architects and engineers, beaver continually change the nature of the streams in which they live. Creating intri-

Get your feet wet. Muddy those hands. By creating or restoring wetlands, especially small wetlands near communities of people, you can give great hope for the future. Here are two stories of wetland projects that were a great success.

A WETLAND CREATED: Students, teachers, and parents at Wolfle Elementary School near Kingston, Washington, decided they needed a wetland after looking at the bare ground surrounding their new school. Instead of building a concrete or asphalt playground surface, wetland biologists helped them design a marsh. They excavated space for a small pond, pumped in water, and planted marsh vegetation that was collected from nearby wetlands and purchased from a wetland nursery. By doing this, the Wolfle Elementary School created their own wetland research center.

A WETLAND RESTORED: Bob Wiltermood looked around his family farm in rural western Washington and thought some things were missing. Wet fields looked to him like they should be much wetter. After a little research and a lot of hard work, Bob began reclaiming a stream, marsh, and pond that had all been largely destroyed by filling and draining.

The first thing Bob did was excavate areas that had been filled. He then planted aspen trees and reshaped a stream channel, lining it with gravel. Water levels soon began to rise in ponded sections of the marsh, and the newly graveled stream flowed clean. Dozens of marsh birds returned to this site, and in what appeared to be a miracle, salmon swam in from the sea and back up and into Bob's streambed to lay their eggs. To look at the marsh today, you wouldn't believe it was ever anything else.

Restoring a wetland is often as simple as digging down to where water waits beneath a covering of fill. A restored wetland might need new plants, and some nurseries now stock them. With permits, you can also collect small clumps of wetland plants from natural locations, such as a marsh, to plant in the restored wetland.

If you'd like to start a project like this with your school or community, look in garden magazines for individuals and companies that could help you. You could also visit garden centers or expositions to try to obtain more information on wetland creation and restoration. Even the smallest corner of a yard can become a wetland now that new landscaping fabrics make it possible to create a marsh. Nurseries sell this fabric that you can use to line a small area that will hold water. Then place some soil, together with a few wetland plants, into the deeper areas. Dragonflies will visit, and maybe a frog or two.

cately fashioned dams of sticks and mud, they store water without blocking the passage of fish. They build sturdy, mound-shaped homes in deep water or burrow into the banks of rivers or lakeshores.

Animals that live in and around beaver ponds include trout, osprey, kingfishers, herons, wood ducks, woodpeckers, frogs, turtles, salamanders, salmon, muskrat, otters, and many more. Trees have been found to grow better near beaver ponds because of the greater availability of water. Salmon populations have been shown to thrive in ponds created by nature's dam builders. Trout anglers often find that fish grow fatter in the beaver's pond because of all the insect life present in these calm waters. But people generally don't appreciate a beaver's work. When a beaver builds a dam that floods a road or field or other area important for people, the first response is typically to tear out the dam. Often, the beaver is also killed.

In our hurry to pave over the world, we have built roads, located farm fields, and paved parking lots in low ground. Low ground today could have been the bottom of a pond years ago. Local conditions of the past often will return. That is exactly what has already happened in many places. Beaver flood low-lying areas when they move back into valleys where they were once trapped out. As they dam streams, water backs up and floods fields, roads, or sometimes even a house.

Beaver were trapped so completely for their dense fur that many areas were nearly without these aquatic animals just after the turn of the last century. Ponds dried up, stream levels changed, and people forgot about the presence of beaver in their area. And people generally have very short memories about the natural world's changes. If beaver disappear from sight, they don't exist in lots of minds. When they come back, it is as if they are here for the first time.

Today, with trapping controlled or stopped, beaver are finally returning to lots of areas, after many years of near

RIVER MODELS

We need models in nature to show us how life should be — what it was like before the riverbank was cleared or the water was polluted. Fortunately, we do have some wonderful rivers and streams in the United States that you will want to visit. You'll enjoy what you find of these flowing waters, and you will see some of the most undisturbed places, not all of which are in national parks.

The following is a list of outstanding streams that exist in areas you can easily visit. They represent a wide range of geographical locations, too:

The Beaverkill, Neversink, Au Sable, and Delaware rivers in New York; the Battenkill River in Vermont; Fishing Creek and Spruce Creek in Pennsylvania; the Quashnet River in Massachusetts; the Housatonic River in Connecticut; the Chattanooga River in South Carolina; the Smith River in Virginia; the Davidson and Nantahala rivers in North Carolina; the Conasauga River in Georgia; the Au Sable and Little Manistee rivers in Michigan; Crane Creek in Missouri; Black Earth Creek in Wisconsin; the Gunnison River and upper Arkansas River in Colorado; the Salmon River of Idaho; the wild and scenic section of the Missouri River in Montana; the Green River in Utah; the Firehole, Gibbon, Madison, and Yellowstone rivers in Yellowstone National Park, Wyoming; the Queets and Quinalt rivers in Olympic National Park, Washington; the Deschutes River in Oregon; the Smith River in California; and a long list of streams in Alaska that could change fast as more people move into that state.

What is needed now is up to you: to make this list as long as possible, making every stream a model of how it should be.

---

extinction. As they come back they probably don't think much of parking lots, roads, or farm fields. They simply go about their business of damming up streams and building their homes; maybe beaver think they have a right to exist.

History can help us see beaver in a different light. An estimated 400 million beaver once lived in North America. This is nearly ten times the number of bison that existed prior to European settlement, and a number that was reduced to near zero by 1900. Today, as beaver return, their numbers are up to about 9 million. As they increase, some people are actually putting them to work to improve streams and vegetation in valleys altered by humans. But people must work with the natural construction behavior of the beaver and understand that their waterworks raise water levels.

Working with beaver means placing bridges in areas where dams back water over roads, rather than paving over small streambeds. It means locating buildings or parking lots above the levels that may be ponded in the future. In general, it means getting to know where beaver are likely to live and to plan accordingly.

BRINGING STREAMS BACK FROM THE DEAD

It may sound obvious that a stream is not a stream when it doesn't flow anymore. Water moving along the ground usually defines a stream, but often that water disappears, sinking into the ground.

Streams vanish for many reasons. The clearing of stream-bank vegetation, trampling of streams and banks by livestock, and destruction of wetlands along a stream will all help dry up a stream. But the water can come back, and many people are helping to bring streams back from the dead.

One of the simplest things to do to help a dry or disturbed stream in an agricultural area is to fence the stream so that cattle can't trample the banks. This simple action has helped many miles of stream recover, even bringing some back after water had completely disappeared.

Replanting trees along stream banks is another great thing to do, but you can usually let nature do this for you. If a stream bank is cleared of all vegetation by livestock grazing, eliminating or reducing grazing will allow plants to grow back on their own. If you do choose to replant, make sure the trees you use are native to your area and adapted to stream banks. Choose aspen, willow, and cottonwood if you are not sure because these trees are widespread natives of stream banks.

There are hundreds, probably thousands, of miles of streams that are unnaturally dry. You can bring them back to life and feel an incredible sense of pride in having restored a stream to its former health.

HOW DO BEAVER HELP US?

Beaver dams slow water movement, creating areas where water is released downstream over time. This helps store water for drier times of the year.

Water from beaver dams also sinks into the ground, slowly adding water in storage areas that many people use for drinking water.

More diverse shorelines and soil conditions cause more varieties of vegetation to grow along beaver ponds than along the remainder of the stream, offering more homes for wildlife. Rich waters are fed by the stream, and the combined effects cause fish to grow larger and have greater amounts of habitat in beaver ponds. This is often critical habitat for fish survival.

Plants growing in beaver ponds and those eaten by the beaver ultimately become cycled into the water as they are eaten by stream insects that eventually become food for fish and other wildlife.

To work with beaver, you can actually attract them as you might attract birds. They won't come flying into your backyard and they won't swim into your pool, but beaver do have one special love in their life. They'll walk a million miles for the sweet taste of aspen wood! If you live near a stream where aspen trees have disappeared, try planting some a distance away from the stream bank. The trees will be eaten, even if you plant them a hundred yards away from the water.

The beaver's love of aspen can even help you create some wonderful wildlife habitat if you have an area that can be flooded. Plant some aspen trees about 50 yards from a stream, and you may encourage beaver to dig a channel over to the trees. If you plant a patch of a dozen or more trees, this may even invite pond construction. Keep in mind, however, that beaver don't like stream areas that are very steep. If the stream is falling over riffles—broken water that tumbles—you're probably not going to attract a beaver. If the water is fairly slow moving, your chances are much better.

In many states, you can even request a beaver from the state wildlife agency. Just like ordering a pizza, you can actually have one delivered. Since many people ask wildlife agencies to livetrap beaver from their streams, these animals can be brought to a stream of your choosing. Just find one with no beaver, ask for a transplant, and you may create some wonderful habitat while giving a beaver a new home.

Lakes and Ponds

You can swim in them, fish from their shore, or sailboard out across their surfaces. Some still sparkle as clean as when your grandparents were young. Others suffer gross neglect. Still others are some of the best examples of ecological restoration we have to offer. Lakes and ponds have one main thing in common, though, and it usually gets them in some kind of trouble when people come near—their water just sits.

Still waters in the modern age are an invitation for disaster. Pollution washes off the land, and falls out of the air. We drop junk into these waters. We pump guck through our pipes and into our lakes. We spray poisonous chemicals, all of which sit in our lakes until something suffers. Amazingly, we even drink water from lakes filled with pollutants.

The simplest example of how we mess with lakes is also one that offers a lot of hope for ways to help them. The example has a lot to do with lake food. When a lake is stuffed with too much food, as if on a permanent Thanksgiving holiday, it is said to be eutrophicated—*eu* meaning "a lot of" and *trophic* meaning "food."

Some lakes are naturally eutrophic because many nutrients wash into them. You can usually identify these lakes by the presence of lots of plants along the shore and quite a bit of blooming algae and other floating plant life in the lake itself. All lakes have their own natural levels of nutrients entering from the land or from wetlands along their edges, as well as from rivers and streams.

When a lake gets really stuffed with nutrients, or becomes

unnaturally eutrophic, it begins to have serious problems. Plants start growing in the lake, and as they die you can smell them rotting. The odor may be unpleasant, but it is not as severe as the impacts rotting plants can have within the water. Often, these rotting plants use up the lake's supply of oxygen as they decay. With lower levels of oxygen, fish begin to die. The cycle continues until the sources of extra nutrients are shut off. .

Saving lakes from eutrophication is often a matter of finding the nutrient sources and diverting them in other directions. But there is one truth in ecology that is worth remembering: There is no such thing as a free lunch. So when the nutrient source is diverted, we must be careful that it does not become something else's problem.

One of the best examples of this can be seen in Lake Washington, which borders the city of Seattle, Washington. For many years, sewage was pumped into the lake, and it became nutrient enriched. As a result of studies to figure out what to do about the eutrophic conditions, a new sewage system was created. Sewage was diverted from the lake, which soon became clean once again. That cleanliness comes at a price, however.

Sewage once pumped into Lake Washington now enters Puget Sound. Although the sewage is more thoroughly treated than when it fouled the lake, it still contains pollutants. Consequently, Puget Sound has severe pollution problems, some of which can be blamed on the sewage.

Everywhere in America, the problems of lakes are similar. Thousands of lakes are eutrophicated by human wastes, as sewers and septic tanks leak into them. Another common problem that is easily avoided is the growing of lawns right up to the edge of lakes. Lawn clippings, fertilizers, and chemicals wash directly into the water, causing eutrophication.

Ever jump into a lake and have the feeling that the creature from the Black Lagoon was tugging at your legs? Chances are that the creature was actually a plant created by lawn fertilizer. Enriched by the lawn runoff, lake-edge plants grow thicker than normal. People then buy chemicals to kill the plants, but the problem is never solved. The best solution is to find the source of unnatural nutrients and divert it, preferably at minimal risk to another lake or wetland.

Another major pollutant of lakes and ponds is acid rain. It is especially harmful to them because the water is captive. Smoke from factories and car exhaust contain acids that rise, then fall, contaminating still waters.

Along the shores of lakes and ponds, the most severe problems arise when we clear away plants, build docks, or construct breakwaters and other shoreline structures. Destruction of this valuable edge between land and lake takes away critical wildlife habitat and removes the lake's defense system. The plants along the shore not only provide homes to animals; they protect the shore from erosion, trap sediments and pollutants, and help modify floodwaters.

For many people, the lakeshore is as special as that of the sea. No matter where you live, you probably are not far from a pond or a lake. Visit there throughout the year and you may see some spectacular wildlife. Watch especially for the one symbol of freshwater wilderness that will call to you when it returns to its own special lake, the loon.

Loons

Once you have seen them dance, you will want to join their lake ballet. They are spectacular, even when they are not up on their feet in their water-walking dance routine. It is no wonder that loons have long been the symbol of northern wilderness.

There are several kinds of loons, and the one we think of as a lake dweller in the United States is called the common loon. The loons communicate with one another in a complex

THE HAZARDS OF NESTING ON WATER

Imagine you're a loon. You build your nest in the same place you did last year and the year before that. It's a job that takes you away from fishing for your dinner, but it is a good thing for raising a family. That way, there will be loons in the future. Besides, the little loon chicks are cute. They even like to ride on your back!

You finish the nest and lay your first egg, but you soon discover that water is pouring in from all sides. The lake is rising. Your nest is flooded.

Loons, ducks, grebes, swans, rails, coots, blackbirds, marsh wrens, and other aquatic wildlife all face this problem. It occurs when people build dams on outlet streams or at the point where lakes pour into a river. The dams raise the water level in a lake, and nesting on the water becomes a disaster.

The most difficult places for wildlife are along the shores of reservoirs — artificial lakes that flood valleys unnaturally. There are hundreds of thousands of acres of reservoirs in the United States. They pose problems to loons and other animals in need of homes, especially when their water levels go up and down. In many cases, habitat that is flooded by the rising reservoir waters is the kind most needed. Wetlands in low-lying areas are the first to disappear beneath the water, and they are the most difficult to reestablish since reservoirs usually are not designed to allow wetlands to grow back. Their unusually steep shorelines offer little room for wetland plants and wildlife.

If you are a loon, you can hope that someone will make a place for you to nest.

voice pattern. Their calls can be a threat, as when they sing in a shrill tone during the dances they perform while running across the water. These threats are usually made if loons try to set up a nesting territory on a lake already claimed by another pair.

Large and heavy bodied, loons easily sink beneath the water to search for prey that includes fish, crayfish, salamanders, and frogs. They need crystal-clear water so they can see to catch their dinner. They also need unpolluted water so that enough prey is available for themselves and their young. Even when the water is clean and clear, loons do not nest if people disturb their nesting places while boating, skiing, or fishing. Loons need lots of privacy.

Loons are among the most fortunate of all wetland animals since they have an organization devoted to them. The North American Loon Fund is a nonprofit conservation group committed to stopping the population decline of loons in North America. They conduct research, publish educational material, sponsor loon meetings throughout the country, and help rally people together in efforts to help the loons.

Members of the North American Loon Fund and other conservationists have pointed out several problems facing lakes and loon populations. One major concern is acid rain. Unfortunately for loons, the lakes most affected by acid rain are also the places where most loon nesting occurs. This area of the northeastern United States and eastern Canada receives high levels of acid rain from urban and industrial areas. Sulfur and nitrogen combine with oxygen to form acids that rise up with smoke from power plants or curl out of car exhaust pipes. Then the sulfuric and nitric acids fall from the sky, raining into lakes and streams where they are deadly to fish.

Some fish, especially trout, are more susceptible to the acid, so the presence of other fish is a good indication that loon populations can be maintained for a while. Loons also can switch temporarily to nonfish prey. But lakes must get rid of the acid to maintain their health over time. This will happen only when industrial sources are cleaned up and automobile emission standards that lower acid production are enforced. Many other countries in the world have acknowledged these pollution problems with actions and laws to protect the air and subsequently lake water.

Other pollutants are beginning to be a major concern as well. Loons are being tested for mercury, PCBs (polychlorinated biphenyls), and other contaminants, and high levels of these toxins are showing up in several areas. The PCB levels are especially critical since they have already affected other aquatic animals, such as seals. PCB is an industrial chemical used for many purposes. Electrical transformers contain the substance, and it was also the compound that made carbonless carbon paper work. It was taken out of the paper, but it is still used in dozens of other products and ends up pouring into lakes accidentally in sewage wastewater. Small amounts can harm wildlife and people, too.

Despite the many problems loons face, their protectors fight for cleaner water, quiet shorelines, and the restoration of wetlands. In New Hampshire alone, loons increased from about 250 in the late 1970s to 400 in 1988. The return of loons to lakes where they had vanished is being celebrated in many other states. Their return is often a direct result of people lending a helping hand.

How can you help loons? One way is to write to your congresspeople, governor, and even the president, asking them to care about clean lakes. More immediate action you can take is to build new homes for these magnificent birds. Loon nesting platforms, like birdhouses on land, have helped lure loons back to many lakes. Loons like small islands, isolated from human activity. When they feel that their nesting site is no longer a safe place, they will leave the lake. If you know of an area that is fairly secluded, especially one where loons used to nest, build a platform and you may see them return. For information on building platforms, write to the North American Loon Fund, 6 Lily Pond Road, Gilford, New Hampshire 03246. Ask also for membership information and for the address of a loon-helping group near your home—many have already been begun.

Trumpeter Swans

Elegant in flight, graceful while swimming, and tough when defending its nest or young ones, the trumpeter is the largest of the swans. Its long neck helps it reach food beneath the surface of the shallow lakes on which it prefers to spend its time. These swans like to eat aquatic plants, such as those found on quiet lakeshores or in marshy areas with some higher, dry spots.

Swans are enormous birds. Their wings are typically wider than those of bald eagles, and it takes a long runway to get them airborne. The 747s of the water-bird world, they flap and paddle to get up and away. This is okay if the swan is out in the water but not so great if it is on land; coyotes can catch them if they can't get into the sky. As a result, swans spend more time on the water than lots of other, smaller waterfowl. They need water not only for food but for safety.

You will not find trumpeter swans wherever the right conditions exist, however. Almost every single trumpeter swan on earth was shot a few generations ago. Near extinction, the swans were finally protected, and they have staged a partial comeback that is often portrayed as one of the best examples of wildlife saved. The trouble is, although we did manage to save the swans, we have done a miserable job of saving their habitat.

The majority of trumpeter swans now living in the lower 48 states are concentrated in and around the Wyoming, Idaho, and Montana area. They nest here, especially in the Red Rock lakes (Montana) vicinity. They also spend the winter in this region, an area that can become very cold, often well below zero. In recent winters, it became so cold that lakes and rivers froze solid and the swans had no place to rest or feed. As many died, people feared that they would become endangered again.

Adding to the harsh winters is another long-term problem the trumpeters face. It is an all-too-familiar one in the West: Water is being taken away from the swans. Just like the fish in many western rivers, swans are losing valuable water they need for winter habitat when farmers withdraw it to irrigate their fields and water their livestock. When this happens, water levels in rivers and lakes drop, making it almost impossible for swans to find areas that are not frozen. Deeper and faster-flowing water can remain ice free, especially where the swans congregate and swim.

The West has also been experiencing a drought that has contributed to the problem of low water levels. This, combined with the swans all living in one major wintering area, has led scientists to move some of the birds to new areas. Swan relocation is helping redistribute them into areas where they may not have such a severe problem surviving the winter. It is hoped that the swans will spread naturally to more areas, reestablishing populations throughout their former range. It is also hoped that farmers will give more water back to rivers.

From 1823 to 1880, approximately 108,000 swan skins, mostly of trumpeters, were sold to London markets by North American merchants. Swans also were killed and sold for their meat and feathers.

By 1916, the total world population of trumpeter swans was estimated at only about 100, due mainly to hunting. Soon afterward, more swans were discovered in Alaska, increasing the population count substantially. By 1970, an estimated 4,000 trumpeters were believed to exist. Populations have grown somewhat in recent years, but can we ever reach the numbers that existed in the 1800s?

For the most part, states do not try to restore wildlife populations to original sizes. They try only to maintain a level that more or less sustains itself over time. Looking at a map of the distribution of trumpeter swans today is a sad reminder of how much the environment has declined. The map contains a little dot out in the corner of Idaho, Montana, and Wyoming. While those are great places to live, the swans' former breeding and wintering homeland once included almost all of North America.

Why not start a whole new trend in America—restoring

wildlife to their former population sizes! If you live in the Dakotas, Nebraska, Minnesota, Wisconsin, Iowa, Illinois, Indiana, Michigan, Washington, or Oregon, you can ask for trumpeter swans to return. Write to your governor or to the U.S. Fish and Wildlife Service, 1849 C Street N.W., Washington, D.C. 20240, the federal agency responsible for managing swans and other water birds that migrate across state lines.

Turtles

A lake without turtles is like a puppy without a tail. Lakes may not need them to survive, and we probably will survive if all the turtles vanish. But life wouldn't be as much fun. For some people, such as some Native Americans, the turtle is the protector of children. A turtle shell placed over an infant's umbilical cord symbolically shields the child from harm.

Out in the lake, a turtle's shell guards it from harm. But the shell can protect a turtle only from natural threats, not from the dangers inflicted by people that drive them from the shore. There are some lakes, such as the alpine waters, where no turtles live because of natural conditions. Like frogs and salamanders, however, turtles are disappearing from their homes, and when they vanish, we lose a valuable part of lake ecology.

As a good example of what can happen to turtles, it is helpful to look at populations at the edge of their range, or boundary of their natural homeland. Some places in the southeastern United States are home to nearly 25 different kinds of turtles. Each type is often plentiful, and changes in populations are difficult to see. In the northwestern United States, though, there are only 2 turtle species, and changes in their populations are obvious.

Although painted and pond turtles still inhabit lakes in

the Pacific Northwest, it is becoming increasingly rare to find them. They need natural shoreline areas, and destruction of their habitat has eliminated their homes. Mile after mile of lakeshore has been cleared, and homes have been built right up to the edge of the water. Docks have replaced fallen logs along the shore, and bulkheads line the water's edge. Boats are more common than water birds, and lawns cover what were once marshy shorelines or tree-lined coves.

Despite all of this, turtles are survivors. Lakes of any size can be home to turtles. They even burrow down into the muck to spend the winter in shallow lakes or ponds that go dry from time to time. In many areas, the best animal to monitor and study will be a turtle.

Learn as much as you can about the different kinds of turtles in your location. Watch turtles throughout the year, discovering where they spend time during different seasons. Monitor their movements and interactions with other animals. Keep records of your own turtle diaries, adding information about the other lake wildlife you see.

You will probably be tempted to bring a turtle home or to school. Think about this for a while, asking yourself what the turtle needs for a home. If you can duplicate what it needs, go for it. But if you can find its true needs only along a wild lakeshore, try to protect that wetland instead. That way, turtles will survive in the future.

Fish

So many kinds of fish swim in our lakes and ponds. You have probably caught a perch, crappie, bass, or bluegill. Maybe you have landed a trout or a landlocked salmon. More people in our country spend time fishing than doing any other outdoor recreation. And most anglers bring their catch home to eat. It's a scary thought these days.

Fish is healthy food according to most doctors. Low in fat

and high in forms of cholesterol that are good for us, many fish are much better to eat than meat. However, if you take a look at the fishing regulations of many states, you will not think they are such a great meal.

The 1991 Michigan fishing regulations carry strong warnings to all of us. Their public-health advisories warn against eating many kinds of fish from Lake Michigan and other bodies of water. Mainly because of PCBs and mercury contamination, people are warned not to eat more than one large lake trout, coho salmon, chinook salmon, or brown trout each week. In all inland lakes, there is a general warning regarding mercury pollution, suggesting limiting fish consumption to once a week. In Lake Sinclair (Michigan), warnings have been issued to the public, urging that only one of several kinds of fish be eaten each week, including walleye, white bass, smallmouth bass, white perch, rock bass, largemouth bass, and bluegill. Nursing mothers should eat no more than one per month, because the chemicals would be passed to her infant through her milk. A further warning hangs ominously over the future: The Michigan authorities state that once a fish is contaminated, there is no way to get rid of the mercury in its body.

Michigan is not the only state with severe lake pollution problems. Texas closes areas to gathering wild food because of mercury contamination, Washington issues PCB warnings, and Maine waters contain some of the highest levels of PCB contamination in the country.

Maybe instead of issuing fishing licenses, selling fishing poles, and promoting the idea that lakes are great places to live, we should try to do everything in our power to correct these problems.

Lakes are polluted by people who build too close to them and the streams leading into their waters. More and more people crowd the shores rather than maintain protective riparian habitat around the lakeshores. Water retains pollution

RIPARIAN HABITAT

The fudge sauce on the ice cream of the wetland world, riparian habitat is one of the richest places for wildlife. Often just a thin band of trees or shrubs, but sometimes a wide bank of vegetation, riparian habitat is the area that borders rivers, streams, and other wetlands.

Riparian woodlands trace a thin path along streams and rivers. Entire forests of cottonwood and willow can be regarded as riparian habitat in our most arid places. It is often cut down, bulldozed, or otherwise cleared to make it easier for people to get to the water. Riparian trees are valued by loggers because they are special or very tall, having grown up in this unique habitat.

Wherever it is located, riparian habitat needs special care. Many studies have shown that wildlife use riparian areas more than surrounding, drier areas. Animals can find water in streams and shelter in the trees. Some wildlife, like the river otter, spend their entire lives in riparian areas.

Animals that are adapted to riparian living include beaver, osprey, otters, wood ducks, buffleheads, goldeneyes, and yellow warblers. Even bobcats, bears, and other large mammals use riparian areas, following streams like highways while seeking shelter from the plants and trees.

Hike into the mountains of the West, up where snow might still cover the ground in July. Scattered across the mountain slopes, tucked in amongst rocky places, you will find some of the most beautiful of all wet places, the alpine lakes.

High mountain lakes receive their water from melting snow or glaciers. Streams feed some of them and fall from many of them, too. Some alpine lakes are self-contained. They perch like sparkling jewels in the high country where, occasionally, you can still drink from their waters.

In contrast to lakes at lower elevations, alpine lakes tend to be fairly free of life. Few nutrients wash into them, so they have little food to support plants or animals. Aquatic insects are often the major natural predators, but fish and wildlife agencies have carried fish into many alpine lakes.

The largest alpine lake in the world, Yellowstone, is spectacular for many reasons besides its size. Almost all of the animals that ever lived in or around the lake in recent centuries still inhabit it. Grizzly bears catch Yellowstone cutthroat trout here. Eagles, osprey, pelicans, and many waterfowl nest at the lake. Only the wolves that once hunted along the shores are now absent.

If you visit alpine lakes on summer hikes, you can help monitor the health of these special places. It is important to test their acidity (ask your science teacher for some litmus paper — special paper that changes color to indicate acid levels) and to keep track of their frog, toad, and salamander populations. Sometimes, local fishing groups are interested in these data, especially a lake's acidity. Contact a member of Trout Unlimited, 800 Follin Lane S.E., Suite 250, Vienna, Virginia 22180, for ongoing survey information.

when it is not treated as thoroughly as it can be. This happens when too little money is budgeted for public projects such as treatment plants.

You might not be able to completely solve the lake pollution problem by working with friends or classmates on conservation projects. But your generation *is* making choices and taking actions that can help save lakes from further harm. People often don't realize what they've got until it's gone.

The natural world has been destroyed over the years, but you now care more about the earth than any generation that has come before you.

Past generations have not handed you a very clean world, and it is going to be difficult and expensive to clean it up. But, as ecologist and writer Wendell Berry has said, "Ecology is good work." There are many great jobs for you: finding ways to solve the mercury problem, returning wildlife populations to their former homes, and making rivers and streams drinkable once again, for animals and for people.

One way to begin saving wetlands is to choose a wetland and a wetland animal. Take their future into your hands, first by learning as much as possible about them and then by finding ways to help them. It takes only *you* to begin a conservation project, to help protect the wetlands and their wildlife.

Showy Lady's Slipper

Marsh Marigold

Painted Turtle

Largemouth Bass

Red-throated Loon

Many kids are taking field trips to wetlands, cleaning up riverbanks, and enjoying the many animals that live in wet places. Some kids are saving wetlands from destruction, while others are actually creating or restoring wetlands near their homes and schools.

Saving wetlands is not an easy thing to do. Already, most of our country's wet areas are gone or severely polluted. So your job is not a simple overnight task. But helping wetlands just might be the most fun of all your earth-saving activities because you can do it while you wade in rivers, while you watch the dance of a loon, or even while you fish! It sounds odd, but it's true. You can actually keep track of stream life while wading or fishing in rivers and streams. The presence or absence of various species will tell you a lot about the water's pollution levels. And watching for loons and other more visible wildlife will let you know if the wet places you frequent are healthy enough to support their needs.

Find a wetland, stream, or lake near where you live. Adopt its needs as if it were an old friend. Get to know who lives in these wet areas and who's moved away! Join with others to take surveys and censuses. Record the sounds of the wetlands as you've learned to do in the pages of this book. Write letters to government officials if you see problems. Take time to enjoy the beauty of the wetlands that still remain, remembering that future generations will want to enjoy them, too. We have only One Earth. It and the future of our wetlands are in your hands. It is up to you to save and share in that future.

Afterword

Save Our Prairies and Grasslands
by Ron Hirschi
Photographs by Erwin and Peggy Bauer

Stroll the shortgrass prairies of the West, where buffalo grass tickles your bare feet, and prairie dogs, bison, and pronghorn roam free. Work your way east through midgrass prairies in search of elusive sharptailed grouse, sandhill cranes, and big-horn sheep. Finally venture to the tallgrass prairies, where visions of wildflowers can be gathered. Closer to home, behold butterflies and bluebirds in lawn gardens and lush green meadows.

Hardcover Price: $17.95 U.S./$21.95 Can.
Hardcover ISBN: 0-385-31149-4
Trade Paperback Price: $9.95 U.S./$12.95 Can.
Trade Paperback ISBN: 0-385-31199-0

Save Our Forests
by Ron Hirschi
Photographs by Erwin and Peggy Bauer and others

Leave the city woodlands and backyard trees to travel through mountain forests, where grizzlies, elk, and wolves make their homes. Enter an eastern broadleaf forest or explore a southern woodland, where warblers, gray foxes, cougars, and black bears live. Venture deep into an ancient forest in search of tree voles, goshawks, marbled murrelets, and salamanders. Even after you've done all that, the rain forest awaits with its lush greenery, fair flowers, hummingbirds, and butterflies.

Hardcover Price: $17.95 U.S./$21.95 Can.
Hardcover ISBN: 0-385-31076-5
Trade Paperback Price: $9.95 U.S./$12.95 Can.
Trade Paperback ISBN: 0-385-31127-3

Save Our Ocean and Coasts
by Ron Hirschi
Photographs by Erwin and Peggy Bauer and others

Saunter along forested shorelines, where bald eagles and great blue herons fly. Climb the rocky coasts and spy sea otters, puffins, and plovers. Set sail for islands and remote nesting beaches, where roseate terns, brown pelicans, and monk seals live. Venture through the coastal wetlands and soft sandy shores to the homes of manatees, sea turtles, and crocodiles. And if you are really feeling spirited, dive near coral reefs and see sharks in the distance or chart the open waters, where whales roam.

Hardcover Price: $17.95 U.S./$21.95 Can.
Hardcover ISBN: 0-385-31077-3
Trade Paperback Price: $9.95 U.S./$12.95 Can.
Trade Paperback ISBN: 0-385-31126-5